MORETHAN

AN

ATHLETE

POEMS BY

ETANTHOMAS

Moore Black Press
Dedicated to Legacy since 1971

Moore Black Press
P.O. Box 10545
Atlanta, GA 30310
404 752 0450
www.mooreblackpress.com
mooreblackpress@yahoo.com

Editor: jessica Care moore-Poole
Art Director: Marcia Jones
Original Cover Art –Marcia Jones
Front and back cover graphic design: Salah Ananse
Front and back cover Photography - Michael Angelo Chester
Book layout and design - M. Chester
MBP Marketing Director-Patrick "the man" Oliver
ISBN: 0-9658308-9-6
Library of Congress Cataloging in Publication Data
Available from publisher
Thomas, Etan; Poetry.
10 9 8 7 6 5 4 3 2 1

CONTENTS

Dedication   VI

Forward by Abiodun Oyewole   VII
The Last Poets

Author Intro
Why I Write/Poetics   VIII

My First Love   2

My Heritage   5

Brotha Malcolm   9

Moses   11

The "N" Word   13

The Good News   16

Toys R Us Kid   18

A Field Trip   21

Haters   24

Aborted   26

Life Doesn't Stop After Birth   27

Wasted Talent   28

Sesame Street   30

Thuggenometry   32

Republicans   35

Some People Don't Need a Gun to Kill You   37

The Know It All   40

Babies Having Babies 43

The Handshake 46

Nightwalker 48

An Abusive Situation 49

True Friendship 52

Alone 56

Trust 58

Karma 60

Return of the Warrior 63

Bring Our Heroes Home 65

Cockroaches 68

The Murder that Murder Produced 70

Please Don't Think I Forgot 74

A State of War by Julian Thomas 77

How Am I Worthy? 79

Ten Poems I haven't had a chance to write yet 81

Publisher's Note 83

Other books from Moore Black Press 84

Mooreblacknotes 85

Discography 86

Dedicated to...

I'd like to thank God for giving me the strength to
endure and overcome any and every obstacle in my life.
I'd like to thank my mother for giving me the
foundation and blueprint to becoming a man. I'd like
to thank my Grandparents for showing me how beautiful
a successful marriage can be (50 years), my wife for
being by my side and supporting me through every
aspect of my life, my brother for giving me the
inspiration to tap into all of my gifts, and every
writer, poet, activist, public speaker that inspired
me to always stand up for what i believe in.

ForeWord By
Abiodun**Oyewole**

I t was in Greenwood, Oklahoma where I first met Etan. Poets, Amiri and Amina Baraka, legendary dance choreographer, Chuck Davis, *The Renny Harris Dance Troupe* and The Last Poets were scheduled to perform at the Greenwood Cultural Center. Some years ago, Greenwood was nicknamed Little Africa or Black Wall Street. It was a very prosperous section of Tulsa developed by Blacks and Native Americans. It is also important to note that Greenwood is the sight of the first domestic bombing of a town in America by other Americans. In 1921, two planes dropped a bomb each on the thriving town. On display in the center are pictures of charred bodies, bombed homes and dreams gone up in smoke. Over six hundred Black business were destroyed.

When I recall the pictures and stories of this horrendous racist attack, a chill comes over me even now. It was after *The Last Poets* performance that I was introduced to Etan Thomas. While I was on stage, I saw him in the audience and I knew who he was because I'm a serious basketball fan and Etan is a serious basketball player out of Syracuse University now playing with the Washington Wizards of the NB A. When the game is played right and the creativity is allowed to flow, B-ball is poetry in motion. Etan stood out. I guess he couldn't help that standing six feet ten inches tall. He was at this high-powered revolutionary concert with his mother who was the one who introduce us. Etan seemed thrilled to meet me and I was as thrilled to meet him.

My son Oba is a Syracuse all sports fan. I think its because Jim Brown and a host of other great athletes like Donavan McNabb, we place Syracuse high on the list, especially when it comes to sports. The most interesting part of our conversation was to discover that Etan had as much passion for poetry as he did for playing ball. We exchanged numbers. I told him if he wrote something and wanted to run it by me give me a call. It just so happened I had a radio gig in D.C. at Howard University's radio station, WHUR, a few months later. I called Etan and told him I was coming to town to do some poetry on the radio and if he wanted to be my guest he was welcomed.

Conscious poetry was the theme and Etan came packing. I was taken back a bit to hear his poetry, like bareknuckles, no gloves to soften the blows. In some cases, it was like he put brass knuckles on his pen - especially when speaking about the hipocricy of democracy and the republicans republic. "I'll tell them *no* child should be left behind then take more money out of schools, I'd show *them* the nightstick and plungers pepper spray and stun guns-you have to eliminate the source of the problem not punish the victims of it."

What was more surprising, is Etan knew his poetry by heart. He didn't read from a paper. He did it live! So when I was asked to write this foreword, I felt it was not only an honor but an opportunity to express my appreciation to Etan and all the other sisters and brothers for not staying locked in the box that someone else designed for you. Finding a way to fly in a productive space of your choosing is a real act of freedom. The poems that follow weren't written by a basketball player. They were written by a man who loves and cares for himself and his people.

Abiodun Oyewole
The Last Poets

Why I write

So many people are taken back by the idea that I write poetry. I often wonder why. Is it because I am a 6'10 Black man who plays in the NBA? Is that all people see when they look at me? If that is, then they don't truly see me. Basketball is something that I love to do, but it isn't all that I am. I laugh when people tell me things like "you speak so well" as if I'm suppose to take that as a compliment. What voice were they expecting to come out of my mouth? Too many times in society, we allow others to dictate what box we are suppose to be in. From they way we dress, talk, think, act, the music we listen to, the movies we watch. We are all in our own little box. Well, I refuse to allow anyone to put me in a box. I have many interests, and poetry is high on that list.

I use poetry for many different reasons. Sometimes, it's therapeutic. A way to get your frustrations out in a positive way. Some people hit a heavy bag, some drink their sorrows away, while others sing the blues. I write. It's a good way to get things off of my chest.

I use poetry to tell my opinions on different topics. I am kind of a throw back type of an athlete in that I am not afraid to stand up for what I believe in. I use poetry as a vehicle to speak out on different issues as you will see later on in this book. From the war, to affirmative action, to the death penalty, to education. There really aren't too many topics that I am afraid to touch. My willingness to speak out on different issues have opened doors for me that I would have never thought possible. From the ACLU, to the NAACP, to the National Coalition To Abolish The Death Penalty to the Democratic National Committee. Who knows where this can take me. I really believe that this is only the beginning.

I also use poetry to tell other people's stories. A lot of times I will have conversations, interactions, or experiences that weigh heavily on my mind. I am and always have been an observer. A lot of times, I will tell other people's stories with my writing. By attempting to put myself in another person's shoes, I become that person in my poem. In poems, such as, *"An Abusive Situation"*, *"Moses"*, or *"Karma,"* I try to explore every avenue of their situation in an attempt to actually feel their pain. To see it through their eyes.

 More Than An Athlete

I also use poetry to speak to young people. This is a real passion of mine. I use poetry as a channel to connect me to the youth of the world. I don't tell them anything that their parents, teachers, or preachers, haven't been telling them most of their lives. The people who kids usually pay the most attention to are athletes, entertainers, rappers, actors, etc. I don't care what Charles Barkley says, I am a role model whether I want to be or not. I use my position as an athlete as a platform. Providing a positive message to young people. Kids know more nowadays that most of their parents can even imagine, and if I can be a positive light for them, I will.

It's funny because when I talk to a lot of young people, they are so afraid to be themselves. They want to conform to what is "cool". I had a young boy ask me why I don't wear any jewelry and why in the world do I have beads on. He told me that I needed to floss like Jay-Z, and I didn't even have a watch on, let alone one "surrounded with so much pink ice". That almost broke my heart because I've never thought along those lines. From the time I was little, I always wanted to be different. If everyone liked one particular style, I wanted my style to stand out. I never wanted to be like everyone else. For many young people, it's just not cool to be interested in poetry. Now sports, hip-hop, cars, ice, those are well accepted interests, but poetry? I encourage young people to be themselves no matter what anyone thinks of them. Don't follow the crowd, be original and stay true to yourself. As long as you are happy with who you are, and you keep God first, no one else's opinion really matters. That is a philosophy that my mother instilled in me at a very young age, and those are words that I live by.

Etan Thomas

PoeticsIntro:

As I extract words from my brain cells
I overwhelm minds with rhymes of a poetic content
Transforming phrases to ideas
Influencing thought patterns
Aimed to challenge mental positions infatuated
I stay frustrating MC's
My flows is levitated
Exasperating metaphors and similes
I'm verbin
Mums the word when
I let loose
Throwing lyrical darts at my victim
Steam rolling my caboose
I may sound mad
I'm not the type of cat to step back and blast
But I will take this pin and punctuate the masses
Don't laugh
This is for real
These flows attack
Cats minds are sacked
Like quarterbacks
Sent into uncommon realms like heart attacks
As the beat goes on
While brothas be babbling
My lyrics is travelin through the air
Like a javelin
And stab you in the abdomen
Just to get my point across
Can you dig it
I'm looking to strangle you
Better yet dangle you
Have you desperately hanging on my every word
Inhale these metaphors while you choking on my adverbs
I'm not cocking pistols I'm cocking ball point pins
Spoken word and written thought
Let the revolution begin

You're not going to reduce me to an entertainer. I'm a man who stands up for what he believes in, and you're going to respect me for it.

—Bill Russell

My**first**love
(Basketball)

F eenin for her touch I got a jones that won't turn back
Not that Lorenz Tate jonin for Nia Long
But like that junkie jonin for that crack
I think I'm hooked
Everlasting crush since six years old
She kept me crunk
Filling me with dreams and aspirations
I see pots of gold at the end of rainbows
Mountains to climb that never seem high enough
Cuz I can taste the sweet butterscotch flavor of victory
Many mysteries go unsolved to the magnitude of our closeness
Everyday I feen to stroke you and feel your curves run through my fingertips

Dreamin of ways to send you through interwoven string
Your connection with my wrist

Sends my mind to an abyss of metamorphic contemplation
Creation of thoughts while giving birth to my dreams
You fill me with hope
Breast-feeding me with possibilities
I'm seeing lights at the end of tunnels
My vision remains un-blurred
My spirit is a glowing florescent light
Burning with a dream un-deferred
Thoughts are blowing through my mind like a whirling durbish

I believe

I believe like God believed in Adam
Like Moses believed he could split the red sea
So I force you through the circles of life
At velocities higher than thermonuclear breakdowns
Bangin you on floors, I mean no harm
Brothas try to prove they can take you away from me
Snatch the ground right from under you and bounce you to the beat of their drum
Heated like a boiling pot of water when I see brothas swarm around you
Yearning to be down with your rhythms
Makin passes to your tune
Swivelin their hips to the bop of your beat

I make them bleed like hemophiliacs with connections of elbows to noses
I leave them stuck like a wack MC with no rhymes
Journeying through space and time
Held motionless
Drownin in an abyss of despair
Gaspin for air
Blinded to the sight of my vision
Illusions of grandeur
Bobbin and weavin through obstacles in my path
Throwing left hooks and jabs
Bitin off ear loaves of Holyfield's that stand in my way
I'm a bomb
My blood boils with nitro-glycerin
No retreat no surrender
My back against the ropes
Dyin to quit but refusing to lose
Like Meth my third eye seen it comin before it happened
Satin sheets and pillows with feathers tickle my imagination

I see you in my sleep possessing the key to success
In line with your rhythmic tune
I read you like a psychic predicting my future
On my mind like ash on a wednesday
Like freedom to kunta kente, I'll never let you go
Physical fixations are manifested
Through closed eyes I can see your presence
I'm constantly pursuing your touch
Like a lion to a cheetah
Ever growing indignation flows through the veins of those you've rejected
But we stay connected
Harmonious sounds are produced over instruments unheard
Smoother than a miles davis blue note
You make me feel I can leap tall buildings in a single bound
Still there's that constant enemy
Planting notions of wasted motions in my ears
Drummin up ideas of the misguided plenty that have fallen by the waste side
Reached for that star but found nothing in their hands but empty promises
Hopes and dreams deferred
A blurred vision to their rhythms

But as the haters grow like weeds in an open forest
My undying love for you stands taller than three Eifle Towers
As I shower opposing forces with the scorching hot burden of proof
I must prove my ability to avoid the failures of the past
This relationship takes practice
Seeking the wisdom to make this thing work
The vision of success makes my eyes grow fonder
I'm almost here
It's right over there
Right within my reach
My eyes saw it like Dionne Warwick
Brought to my existence like the three kings bearing gifts of wisdom
More times than Jimmy Swaggert begging for forgiveness
The world is mine
Thanks to my
first
love

I've discovered my heritage
My great grandmother from Grenada
My great Grandfather from St. Croix
I have spice running through my veins like a dread in Babylon
Placed upon my head like an African crown
I stand as proud as a king

A warrior
Basking on the beaches of the West Indies
After the morning gathers the rainbows
The shores are dripping wet with beauty
The sun descending as the night rose
Lingering aromas of tranquility
I can smell your scent with my eyes closed
The moon's reflection on the waters of the night
As everything is always irie in my Caribbean paradise
The love of my land is as solid as a rock
So guess who's coming to dinner?
Notty Dreadlock
Out of the filth and slime of slavery rose a sentiment so pure
so without anger
so full of love
As Bob Marley speaks to me through redemption songs
Telling me that one good thing about music
is when it hits you feel no pain
so hit me with music
That natural mystic
Blowing through the air

Peter Tosh sets my eyes toward the mother land
Home of the Lion Of Judah
I embrace the culture like a newborn baby named Gingy
Holding it close to my soul
Feeling the heartbeats and rhythms that drum to the beat of Ras Tafari
Don't let them fool you
Righteousness is the peace I find within in my pride
Don't let them change you
Or even rearrange your freedom of spirit
As serenity overtakes I and I
Wearing my locks with pride

An extension of everyting natural
Staying connected to the Most High
Remaining humble is never deemed impractical

My Locks
Remind me of who I used to be
And the man I will become
My roots and my future
They remind me of my patient dedication to my dreams
They remind me of my inseparable bond between my family
My woman
And myself
Yes, they remind me of myself
My bond within myself
And my own isolated space in the universe
They remind me of a softly setting sun
Casting shadows on a cool drinking hole
At dusk
They remind me of children
Black children
Naked and unashamed
Untainted
Cloaked in the warm gentle breeze
Of a grassy plain
They remind me of music
A calypso hip-so beat
Backed by the effortless rhythms
Of an easy skankin singer
They remind me of youth
Strong and unaware
Boldly and blindly going
Where they've never dreamt of before
They remind me of the earth
Filling my splayed fingers
With handful after handful
Of the rich brown soil
I was one with the planet
Could barely keep my balance as it shifted

Never drifting away
I stayed connected like a square
A lifted symbol on public display

I'm from the home where a full figure
is no sign of shame
where the dignified style is a lion's mane
no cd roms or flat screen graphics
in digital high speed
just a family dinner of curry and plantain
and the tide of the ocean to lull us to sleep

the way mother nature intended
my spirit is my guide and it speaks to me daily
at night i grow wise by my ancestral memory
it was they who taught me how to

listen
listen
listen

and to hear
the pulse of the earth like a drum line snare
starching my back, as it whistles the air
telling the story of every drenched brow
every war torn husband that was made to bow down
every back broken father, snatched from his farm

we are your children
our lives are your psalm
a unified voice
and a unified song
as long as we live on
they will always live on...

they live on

co-written by Julian Thomas

> *"He made us feel holy and he made us feel whole. He made us feel loved and that we were worth something finally on this planet.*
> —*Sonia Sanchez*

BrothaMalcolm

Labeled anti-Semitic
You weren't accepted by the mainstream media that tried to lynch you
                                          on paper

You worshiped Allah
So the Christian Black folks couldn't hear the truth
                              you spoke daily
Once existing as Little
your world was turned upside down right before your eyes
A prince in the making
Minds you were shaking
Sending trembles of fear through the hearts of the oppressor
Gave us all tickets past the promised land but we refused to go
Didn't know the many ways the angels were in disguise because
our eyes were closed
We couldn't see the horns protruding from the heads of the snakes
slithering through our every existence
As constant as the night ends
We continued to clash like titans over conflicting methodologies
As secret societies arose aimed at your destruction
You showed us the stars and stripes that bore witness to our retched condition
While remaining in submission to a higher being
The truth you were seeing
Refusing a dictator's settlement
Arrested was your development
As your eyes had seen the glory
Through the darkness of evil you remained as bright as the shining sun
The pathological one
Moses ready to lead his people to freedom of the mind, body and soul
The captain of a ship Elijah saw and new
However existing as Judas in the eyes of a few
But you stayed on point
Continuing sequels of mental resurrection
Launching a cultural revolution to un-brainwash our people
Gave us protections of armor through lessons of pride
You saw the light in the midst of tunnels consumed with a blond haired
                                          and blue-eyed darkness
You injected the truth into the veins of the multitudes pulling the wool
off the eyes of the masses

Existing in a state of vanglorious
Our minds were protected by your knowledge of self
Force feeding us with wisdom enabling our minds to grow stronger

by any means, you deemed it necessary

for Black Women to be put on pedestals
high as the heavens
While covering their prized possessions as precious temples
Told us that respect should be demanded
Since it was never handed freely
Taught us that education was our future
and that tomorrow belongs to those who prepare today
Instructed us how to love ourselves while rejecting the enemy's ways
You soaked our minds with wisdom and pride
Conceptualizing ideas to life
Wetting more heads than John the Baptist
Your words would shower our realities
You kept us thirsty for more
Opening doors that we couldn't conceive were able to budge
Breaking down the barriers once sealed shut
Unlocking the prisons our minds were trapped in
You possessed the key
We needed you

You're legacy will always live on
We will never allow the light of your fire to be extinguished
Continuing your plan
Never forgetting your lessons
Walking with our brothas hand in hand
For the rest of eternity
You will always remain

The Black Shining Prince of our land

Moses

inspired by a conversation with a **homeless man**

I dwell in dark desolate areas
The stench of piss and garbage stain my flesh
The funk of my horizon lingers in the air
My mind is running ramped like the mad hatter
As I scatter through garbage cans in search of a bite to eat
When will I meet the end of my rope?
When will the sand in my hour glass exceed its limit?
Avoiding gimmicks and cons
My hand is held flat   out
in the begging position

Noses are turned in disgust as mistrust
is filled in the many passersby
I see fear in their eyes
They panic like they're holding a bomb
on a 20 second timer

Why am I the one despised?
Feared?
The degenerate?
The shame of a nation?

My mind travels through a whirlwind of contemplation
Why won't God answer my prayers?
I squeeze my voice box `til it lets out hypnotic melodies
Traveling through the air with the power of Pavoratti
While the pain of famine runs through my body
like a cancer
I still get no answer from the man upstairs

Maybe he don't have call waiting to be waiting on my call

Or maybe my life ain't worth 6 pents
I'm yearning with desire
My mind desperately aspires to be set free
I'm shouting to the heavens above
Lord why hath thou forsaken me?
In these last Babylonian days

More Than An Athlete 11

I can't taste the joys of life
They're not within my reach
Trapped in a hopeless mind state
I cause commotions as stares pierce through my soul
I'm caught up in some elm street dream
And to get the hell up, I must wake up my any means
But I'm stuck
My position remains unchanged

In this tug-of-war of life
No matter how hard I pull
I still land face down in the mud
Everything fails with the unfortunate
These cardboard boxes don't work in the winter time
My life is filled with stressful days
And nights cold as ice
I wish I could turn back the hands of time
Return to the womb of my creator
Then I could feel the warmth of love
And hunger wouldn't strangle my ever being
With the strength of Othello's hands
Or maybe I could paint the world a portrait of my mind
with Michelangelo brush
Showing scenes of pain
Episodes of incurable heartaches
Searching for an exit out the frame
My spirit is leveled like the rain forest
A ghetto prisoner unable to rise
I'm forced to despise my every existence
I drown my sorrows in bottles of poison
Contemplating suicide
My voice begins to sing…

Somehow
I will go on

  More Than An Athlete

The"**N**"Word
(After Randall Kennedy)

Taming, civilizing, and minimalizing the filthiest, dirtiest,
and nastiest word in the human language

Cats be using this word as a term of endearment
Forgetting how they been spearing our ancestors with these six letters
Rolling so easily off their tongues since they stole us from our native lands
Pressed into the depths of our minds by wicked hands
Drowning in a never ending quick sand of hate
It exists as a scar from centuries of racism refusing to heal
A full course meal of poison served fresh
Employed to impose installments of an inferiority complex
Why won't we let this word die?

How can it still caress our everyday lives
Massaged into young minds while creating mental genocide
Murdering the pride our ancestors died fighting for
Destroying the mind our forefathers tried defending
Ignoring the cries our people suffered

The stolen dignity

Subjected to the pain of oppression
Injected with the stain-forced negativity
Still unable to wash our minds clean
Ridding it of the filth of a soiled self-esteem

Now, we don't see it as being that serious
Civilizing the work of barbarians
They minimalize it with ridiculous notions
Drinking potions of hypnotic contempt for themselves

Different spellings
Meaning different things

As the argument goes
We can take the power away and make it our own
Forming some non-derogatory version
Ignoring the history of its undertones

Screamed into microphones nationwide
Blistering sounds piercing the ear on every street corner
Plagiarizing fools copy what they view
dummy see   dummy do

Ignorant mind states created
Once stronger than steel become heavily sedated
Duplicated eyes seeing the word as a magic sword only cutting
in the hands of certain people
They think the word doesn't offend, but only the person does
The hatred for the history of the word becomes lost like self pride
As a word aimed to dehumanize becomes part of everyday language
I stand mesmerized at how a word once a signal of hostility became a term
announcing affection
A piece of clay shaped into different meanings
I'm only seeing one way to view a swastika
Or a confederate flag

But I digress

Some don't even have a problem using it in the presence of pale ears
Fountains of ignorance spews out of their mouths
From salutations to possessions
Recurring sessions of contradictions
Mastered art of perfecting negativity
Unenlightened masses take part in self -denigrating classes
And are even too blinded to get offended when talented white rappers use it in
lyrics!
They stand unaffected and accept his weak apologies
Pretending like nothing ever happened
And all is forgiven
When it can flow from colorless lips
Roll off foreign tongues and objections are not thrown
Something is terribly wrong
I disagree with Randall Kennedy's assertion that we should convert the word
from a negative to a positive appellation

Why would I make their hate suit me?

Pulling up a chair to their table of stupidity
Accepting the unacceptable
The enemy's dream should have been deemed impossible
How can we fail to reject their views of our secondary class of existence
Seeing our self worth through their eyes
Embracing a word aimed to teach us to despise our own reflections
Their whips have scarred our minds as well as our backs
If we don't respect ourselves
How can we expect anyone else to?
Even educated fools
should be smarter

than

that

The**Good**News
(missionaries)

"I love the pure, peaceable, and impartial Christianity of Christ. I therefore hate the corrupt, slaveholding, women-whipping, cradle-plundering, partial, hypocritical Christianity of this land."
                                                                    —Frederick Douglas

They've traveled to foreign lands
Bringing what they call the good news
Amused and amazed at the existence of people dwelling in darkness
Without the sparkplug of rosary beads
And absent of hail marys
It's their duty to scream
let there be light

Giving sight to the blind
Resurrecting the souls of a people lost at sea

The Good News!

In the form of food and schools
They dangle the picture of a better life in front of their faces
Showing endless possibilities if they only walk toward the light
Bread crumbs leading to the throne of alters
encompassed by holy water and prayers of
"Our Father who art in heaven"
But whose kingdom is coming?
And whose will is being done?
Bombarding them with pictures of a
Blond-haired, blue-eyed Jesus
and angels with similar features
Creating creatures of fiction seen through *their* eyes
Teaching them to despise themselves
Disguising evil intentions with acts of kindness
And they have fooled many
Proceeding to pin perceptions
Peeling away at the soul of their protective crown of truth
Once worn around their heads to ward off evil spirits
Bob Marley warned of the ways of the wicked
Vaticantly

Catholisizing
Anglican ways

They've searched for new prey across the globe

The Good News!

Even if you win, you actually lose
They've contorted religion to serve their hidden agenda
Stapling notions of inferiority into the minds of my people
Christened into a baptismal bliss
Cloaked in priest collars and habits
Their beautiful African names are replaced
Their heritage abandoned
Forced to accept new Christian names
while singing the blues…

The Good News

ToysRUsKid

I'm a Toys R Us kid and I don't wanna grow up
I've seen what it does to folks
Life that is
Or the lack there of
Because love becomes transformed to hate in the minds of grown ups
That's why I don't want to grow up
I'm a Toys R Us Kid
They keep telling us that winners never cheat and cheaters never win
but Florida elections say otherwise
Disguised as democracy it doesn't seem fair to me
That's why, I don't wanna grow up
I'm a Toys R Us Kid
I'd rather play hangman
Than be the young Brotha hung
By Bush's commitment
To capital punishment
Now called *the death sentence*
Avoiding repentance
But able to pull the switch to end a life
Guilty until proven otherwise is the way in the world of grownups
They'll plunge into me with plungers
Plant evidence and
Run to public beatings caught on tape
Get acquitted after
Gracing me with 41 shots into two raised hands
simply because I fit the description

Id rather *remain* innocent than *plead* innocent as a defendant seeking vengeance
and needing repentance because I've fallen into sin and I can't get up

Grown ups
Grown ups are bad
They take things that don't belong to them
Discover places that already exist
Creating their own forms of justice
And cease to creating peace for all
But deem necessary to enslave for their own personal pleasure
And they tell me if I tell

Then I'll go to hell
But I'm already here
So I figure might as well
Be a tattle tell
And tell ya'll that I don't wanna grow up
I'm a Toys R Us kid
And I'd rather play video games and *red light green light*
Tag and peek a boo
Instead of peeking at my wife's Black eye
Hearing her cries
An abundance of hows and whys
Seeing tears stream down her face
Replaced with fear
Cuz she is dead wrong
If she ever forget
That I'm the man of this house!!!
You don't talk to me that way
If I was a grown up that's what I'd say
But I'm a Toys R us Kid
And I don't do those types of things

I like to sing happy songs and skip rocks in ponds
I play with GI Joe and Hulk Hogan Heroes
But, in the world of grown ups...
Unsafe sex causes viruses to be passed like batons
As Morale is sunk lower than the depths of the souls of mischief
Child molesters caught on tape can avoid convictions
and continue making platinum selling records
They'll protect the guilty rich but punish the innocent poor
Sending four or five juveniles to prison for crimes they didn't commit
Labeled as animals as a result of the death of a central park jogger
they had nothing to do with
See, grown ups take oaths of hypocrites
Telling us violence is never the key
Turn the other cheek and never fight fire with fire
But then they knock down doors to start wars
With hands stained by the blood of foreign sands
They murder Iraqi civilians

Occupy lands where an abundance of oil can spoil the plans to rebuild
Zero weapons of mass destruction found can only lead to question marks

Grownups will criticize hip hop for glorifying violence
Then elect governors in the state of California
who got rich by glorifying violence!

In the world of grownups, you can be an incompetent,
conniving, manipulating, murderer, and still be re-elected as
President of the United States of America
But they tell me if I tell
Then I'll go to hell
But I'm already here
So I figure might as well be a tattle tell and tell ya'll
That I don't wanna grow up
I'm a Toys R US kid
I'd rather play hop scotch and skip to my lou
Instead of hopping from bed to bed like the grown ups do
I hate grown ups
The words I Do become meaningless
As people change wives like they change their shoes

See grown ups love to lie, cheat, steal, kill
And still feel that they're real enough to know the deal
& shout Amen on Sunday mornings
Speak in tongues and dance in the spirit
While drowning in sin all the week long
Strong enough to call themselves priests
But weak enough to take advantage of little alter boys
And tell them if they tell then they'll go to hell
Grownups
Grownups are here
Grownups are life
Everything was so much easier when I was a kid
It's becoming harder to remain in the world but not of it
So what am I to do?
Try to keep it real
Yeah, real as these toys I love to play with

A**Field**Trip

I wanna take some cats on a field trip
I wanna get one of those big yellow buses with no air-conditioner and no seat belts
Round up Bill O'Reily, Pat Buchanan, Trent Lott, Sean Hannity, Ann Coulter,
Karl Rove, Dick Cheney, Jeb Bush, Bush jr. and Bush sr., John McCain, John
Ashcroft, Gulliani, Arnold, Katherine Harris, Ed Gillespie, that little bow-tied
Tucker Carlson and any other right wing, conservative republicans I can think of,
and take them all on a trip to the hood
Not to do no 30 minute documentary
I mean drop them off and leave them there
Let them become *one* with the other side of the tracks

Give them four mouths to feed and no welfare
Have scare tactics run through them like a laxative
Criticizing them for needing assistance
Show them working families who make too much to receive welfare
but not enough to make ends meet

I'd employ them with jobs with little security
Let them know how it feels to be an employee at will
Able to be fired at the drop of a hat

I'd take away their opportunities
then try their children as adults sending 13 year old babies to life in prison

I'd sell them dreams of hopelessness
while spoonfeeding their young with a daily dose of inferior education
I'd tell them no child shall be left behind,
then take more money out of their schools
Tell them to show and prove themselves on standardized exams
Testing their knowledge on things they haven't been taught

Then I'd call them inferior

I'd soak into their exterior notions of endless possibilities
I'd paint pictures of assisted productivity
If they only agree to be all they can be
Dress them up in fatigues and boots
With promises of pots of gold at the end of rainbows
Free education awaits to rain on those who finish their bid

Then I'd close the lid on that barrel of fool's gold by starting a war
Sending their unqualified children into the midst of hostile situations

And while they're worried about their children being murdered
& slain in foreign lands
I'd grace them with the pain of being sick and unable to get medicine
Give them health benefits that barely cover the common cold
John Q would become their reality
As HMO's introduce them to the world of inferior care
Filling their lungs with inadequate air
Penny-pinching at the expense of patients
Doctors practicing medicine in an intricate web of rationing and regulations
Patients wander the maze of managed bureaucracy
Costs rise and quality quickly deteriorates
But they say managed care is cheaper
They say free choice in medicine will defeat the overall productivity
As co-payments are steadily rising
I'd make their grandparents have to choose between paying their rent and paying
for their medicine

I'd feed them hypocritical lines of being pro-life as the only Christian way to be
Then as contradicting as it seems, I'd fight for the spread of the death penalty
As if thy shall not kill applies to babies but not to criminals

I'd introduce them to those sworn to protect and serve
Creating a curve in their trust in the law
I'd show them the nightstick and plungers
pepper spray and stun guns
mace and magnums
They'll soon become acquainted with
Shake downs and illegal search and seizures
planted evidence and being stopped for no reason
harassment ain't even the half of it
41 shots against two raised hands, a wallet and cell phone
confused as illegal contraband
I'd introduce them to pigs who love making their guns click like wine glasses
Everlasting targets showered by bullets making them a walking bulls eye
Living Pinatas

Held at the mercy of police brutality
Then we'd see if their eyes weren't finally aware of the truth
Open like a box of pandora
They'll see how the other side of the tracks
carries the weight of the world
on their shoulders
and how society seems to be holding them down with the force of a boulder
the bird of democracy flew the coup in Florida

See, for some, injustice comes in packs like wolves in sheep's clothing
Tko'd by the right hook of life, many are left staggering under the weight of the day
Leaning against the ropes of hope
When your dreams have fallen on barren ground, it becomes difficult to keep
pushing yourself forward like a train
Administering pain like a doctor with a needle
their sequels continue more lethal than injections
and they keep telling us all is equal
I'd tell them that instead of giving tax breaks to the rich, financing corporate
mergers, and under the table dealings with Enron and Halliburton maybe they
could work on making society more peaceful
Instead they take more and more money out of inner city schools, give up on the
idea of rehabilitation, and build more prisons for poor people
Closing the door on opportunities while unemployment continues to rise
like the deficit
they wonder why so many people think crime pays
maybe this trip would make them see the error of their ways
or maybe it's just time to get out and vote
and as far as their stay
                    in the white house
tell them
            numbered
                    are their days

Haters

Dedicated to Doug Collins, the coach who told me i'd never make it in the NBA

You never wanted me to make it
Did everything in your power to conquer my spirit
Inhibit my progress while subduing my strength
Pinching my passion
You wanted me to fail
Fall flat on my face
Fulfilling your wish for my dreams to be deferred
Suffocating my desire to attain my goals
You wanted my aspirations to exist merely as a figment of my imagination
Never to escape into the realms of reality
But only existing within the fantasies of my thoughts
Through cerebral failures you wanted me to experience conceptual breakdowns
To give up on my hopes, kidnap my wishes and steal my desires
Perceptual shake-downs
Why would you aspire to see my universe crumble?
Take pleasure in seeing me stumble off my path
Your prayers conspired against me
Bidding for my downfall
Calling on roadblocks to impede my progress
Knocking me off track
Sending me back to the depths of failure
Where dreams refuse to glow in the dark
Where should have beens ponder possibilities
as opportunities slipped through the cracks of their victory
Backing down their chance at success

You would love for your words to knock me down for the count
For me not to withstand your verbal beat down
For my pride to become swollen shut
In need for my trainer to cut me
Clearing my vision
You wanted to keep me trapped in the loser's box

But like Saul Williams,
"I stopped combing my mind so my thoughts could lock"
I'm so glad I ignored you
Paying you any attention is something I couldn't afford to do
With your fake smiles to lure me into your trust
Busting through walls

More Than An Athlete

I refuse to lose
You can't capture my passion with nets of disaster
I'm avoiding sacks like quarterbacks
Call me Donovan
Side stepping your negative advances

I will never dance to your tune
I'm dismissing your songs of doom
You want them soon to be coming to my theater
To be a box office smash
Crashing my will to succeed

Your shots of destruction can't harm me
My desire is bulletproof
So keep busting at my joy
I'm catching your bullets in my teeth like Bruce LeeRoy
Because I've got the glow of God within me
And prosper not will any weapons formed against me
So put simply,
Your desires for me to fail
will never stop me

Aborted

Abortion is a topic that i struggle with. From a personal standpoint I'm pro-life, and i express that view in "*Aborted*," however, there are many points that people who are pro-choice present that i agree with. I decided to explore the other side of the argument with the poem, *Life Doesn't Stop After Birth*."

Left without continuation due to circumstance
Not given a chance to breathe life.
But lifeless lungs are created
Due to the pro rated rate of increasing pro choice voters
Existing realities of a non-existing state
Evident in a failure to communicate the value of life
Distorted views of a life sentence fail to see the beauty of a new creation
An abundance of excuses from unprepared to a victim of circumstance buzz
around heads like bees around honey
A doomed bundle of joy
Destroyed at the request of its maker
Not given the chance to be a shaker of minds
But destined to be crucified by the powers that be
Mothers using ill forms of contraceptives
Lost in a web of predetermined notions of freedom to choose
death over life
As being an inalienable right
To play God
Lost in a web of confusion
While practicing barbaric resolutions
Women should control their own bodies
but murder is not an option
Extinguishing the fire of life lines
While tossing heart beats in coffins
Showered with flowers at the mantle
as often as allowed
ashes to ashes
Entrusted with rusted hopes
dust to dust
Problemic endeavors overshadow the burning desire to live and be free
freedom from execution/the silenced noise of a child's cry/a smothered
voice/exterminated with a raid anted baby killer/called freedom
of choice

Life Doesn't Stop After Birth

Left without an option while locked in a continual pattern
Spiraling into a battered future
A cycle of poverty and abandonment
Abuse and mistreatment
When sex craved, ill prepared, absent minded teenagers see
one line instead of two
The unfortunate reality of the misguided youth
Uninformed and unequipped
While in hot pursuit of pleasure
However, is the answer to make a bad situation worse?
A child born to the unprepared
While pro-lifers pretend to care
Seemingly unaware that life doesn't stop after birth
Searching for ways to preserve life
But what happens after the unwanted arrive
Where are they then?
When the mother is forced to have the seed of a savage beast
Made to produce the child of a rapist
Who will ease the pain of her stained womb
Erase the thoughts of this sadist/a stolen innocense/a hardened soul/armed with
a constant reminder/who will silence the cries of her heartbeat telling her to
despise this new creation/while protesters bomb clinics

Are they really concerned about saving lives?
Causing young girls to risk their safety in back alleys?
Thrust into the wicked arms of illegal practices
Devoid of ethics/armed with rusted knives/sharpened scapels

Where are they then?

Somewhere harassing young mothers outside of clinics
calling them muderers
They want to bring forth a sentence of everlasting strife
Telling women what to do with their own bodies
While hiding behind the label of being

pro-life

Wasted**Talent**

Yo, I've seen that cat before
He had more handles than Marbury, Iverson, and Skip to My Lou
Couldn't wait to break through and bless the world with his skills
Forget a job, his talent would pay the bills cuz dude had game
Plainer than I could say it
He would rain jumpers like thunderstorms
Would be defenders stood frozen in time
Their strategies remained archaic
He was every coaches nightmare
He defied laws, the rarest form of gravity
Stayed in the air long enough to say five hail Mary's
Cats thought he had wings underneath his jersey
And he could play D
Blessed with the ability to twist bodies like a contortionist
He left top scorers in bondage waiting to be set free
He had the illest moves like crush groove and breakin'
He could shake a brotha right out his shoe laces
I ain't lyin
I've seen him do it
Oohs and Aaaahs fill the crowd as soon as he walked through it
His future looked brighter than the sun's reflection
He connected enough elbows to would be assassins so necks should be protected
His love of the game injected passion into his veins
He created an art form
It was like poetry in motion
He formed masterpieces
School was constantly in session leaving his pupils screaming
teach us teach us
He confused minds with his creativity
as they questioned the possibilities of his talents
College scouts watched on
Their hands over their mouths in amazement
Trying to avoid joining the cheers and shouts of the crowd
because they're supposed to be there doing business
Licking their chops like a predator gazing upon a prey
Drooling like salivary glands, they knew this was collection day
Should he even bother with college, or go straight to the league,
birthed topics of debate
Pre-conceived notions claiming dollar signs over education

occupied his mental state
But how couldn't it?
I mean, this was his dream!
A decision to go pro would cure headaches like aleve
He wouldn't need to stress the strain
that pained the strength of his single mom
struggling to make ends meet
Money would no longer be a problem
Now she could get her jewelry out the pawn shop
Tell her landlord to go to hell
This mirage of happiness saturated his mind
But somehow his train of focus
would soon derail

Choices

His choices would cloud his vision
                    an overcast
Constructions of thunderstorms sending lightning bolts
through his hopes and dreams
His potential remained a mystery
Drugs, guns, and crime occupied his time while quick cash
harassed his concentration
Chasing away his aspirations with a stick of thug life
Hennessy, weed, and money
Sex, greed, and the dummies he called his crew
Blowing a Miles Davis Blue note through his pursuit to happiness
His dreams remained unseen
like weapons of mass destruction
But he continued his productions of self destruction
he fiend for that fast life
It kept calling him and calling him as he longed for one last hit
He made the mistake of using his own product and now he's hooked
lined and quickly sinking
Stinking with the stinch of an addiction he gave it all away
Possibilities of the NBA washed down the toilet of his choices
Now he just sits and nods away
In and out of consciousness
Damn, what a shame

SesameStreet

Sunny days
Sweeping the clouds away
On my way
To where the air is sweet
Won't you tell me how to get
How to get to Sesame Street

The perfect place
The magic carpet ride
Where every door is opened wide
Instead of being slammed shut in the face of reality
Happiness wouldn't be cleverly cloaked in misery's disguise

Oscar wouldn't be a grouch cuz he's sitting in classes that tell him he's less than average
Being taught by teachers with patience shorter than half of a smurf's size
That's where I wanna go
where they won't stick me in special sections if I read too slow
they won't bombard me with labels calling me inferior
The term "at risk" would be non-existent
I'd be showered with positive re-enforcement from head to toe

(The concept seems so beautiful)

Snuffulufugus and Big Bird wouldn't use their size to bully me
My pain wouldn't be their only source of inspiration
I could actually walk the halls, without looking over my shoulder
At every kid who loves to rejoice at my misery
Or enjoys making me cry through episodes of public humiliation
Their laughter wouldn't be directed
at me

Elmo wouldn't be picked on cuz his voice was a little high
They wouldn't bombard him with wedgies, and nookies,
or spitballs, to pass the time
I wouldn't be teased for simply being different
I'd be embraced and my spirits would be lifted
Still seen as gifted because I was talented in my own way
Everybody didn't have to be the same
All of my teachers would actually care about me
Instead of giving up on me so easily
They wouldn't be so quick to suspend me

More Than An Athlete

Instead, they would dig deep
Revive my ability
They wouldn't cast me away
like someone with leprosy
I wouldn't be perceived as a threat no matter what my size
Or see the contempt in their heart and the fear in their eyes
They would actually see me

Where the air is sweet
Where everyone can come and play
And everything's a-ok

I can stay outside at recess without worrying about stray bullets coming my way
Count Dracula wouldn't be adding up how many kids
got shot
at my school

Cookie Monster would only be addicted to cookies
Bert and Ernie wouldn't be threatened by rumors
when nobody knows the truth.
And even if they were, nobody would care
Only God could judge them
and doing His job is something they wouldn't dare

My parents wouldn't be too busy for me
Wrapped up in their careers
I wouldn't be a mystery
My own parents would baby-sit me!
Quality time wouldn't be occupied by strangers
I'd be their number one priority

They'd sing to me as if my name was rubber ducky telling me that
" I'm the one who makes their life lots of fun"
Showering me with kisses and hugs
They would talk to me
Teach me about the birds and the bees
Everything would be so lovely
In this land of make believe
Maybe I need to stop fantasizing
Because Sesame Street
never existed for me

Thuggenometry

Brothers be earning bachelor's degrees in thuggenometry
Embracing the art of criminal mind states
Patterns of illegal endeavors
Never cease to amaze me
Tales of incarceration are glorified
As if "OZ" is an entertaining place to be

Thoughtless actions igniting a crime spree
While mindless contraptions take over destinys

Negative forces yelling charge at the top of their lungs
Murdering their possibilities
Leaving them sprung like coils hanging from Mississippi trees

Yea, we've been done wrong
but we do each other worse

With the appetite for destruction
It brings the eruption of volcanoes
Spewing hot lava of genocide
Thugged out ones
Leading us down paths of unrighteousness

Don't get me wrong
I realize times are tough
While weathering the storm of Bush's plans

Our dreams remain imprisoned, hopeless.
As the ratio of Black and Brown faces
Herded into places of correctional facilities
Happens faster than Olympic races

Striking crushing blows to the struggle

Revolutionaries are muzzled
Black minds are puzzled
As the inmate population continues to grow
Never sewing the wombs of oppression
But taking part in incarceration sessions

But, who's to blame?
Yeah, we're targets
And to them our skin is our sin
But why fall into traps set by predators
if we can see it coming from a mile away?

day after day

We won't get a fair trial
That luxury doesn't apply to us
So who can we trust?

Ourselves?

"I have more respect for a man who lets me know where he stands, even if he's wrong, then one who comes up like an angel, and is nothing but a devil."

—Malcolm X

Republicans

(**Affirmative**Action)

Them hypocrites don't care about you
They're just out to rescue their mission
They sing renditions
Of being for the people
But they're sequels are everlasting
The rich get richer
And the poor don't get a damn thing
So how do they keep getting re-elected?
They take my people's dreams and wreck it
Got me wondering where funding is coming from for my future children
Unless I shell out dollars and dollars for some overpriced
private school
Their education's not valued
White kids in the suburbs get new books and computers
They get tutors and mentors to help them with algebraic equations
While they cut the budgets of inner city schools
Negating attempts to rescue young black minds

which are a terrible thing to waste

Cats in the hood be sharing used books
Expected to overlook the 40 nappy heads packed into classrooms like slaves
While underpaid, unappreciated teachers attempt to communicate
to the masses of minds
It's a crime
They have Masters in Criminology
Where air-conditioning is considered a luxury
Must be bad luck to be
Born on the wrong side of the tracks
Lost in the cracks of society
Strategically placed at the end of the labor line
And Bush said, *"No child shall be left behind"*
If dollar signs don't grace your wallet
Education can't grace your mind
While standardized tests compare the suburbs to the inner city
Advantaged to the disadvantaged
They label us inferior
You think that you can judge my mind when you can't read my thoughts
Test scores don't measure future performance

Just your ability to take tests
Educated guess work
Tricks and trades of deductive reasoning
But if the seasoning that you've sprinkled on the school system was equal
Institutions of higher learning wouldn't need methods of special consideration
You have to eliminate the source of the problem
Not punish the victims of it
Reverse discrimination!

Are you serious?!

You've started a race at a pace thousands of spaces in front of your opponent
How many advantages do you need?
Then you recruit black faces to join you in your absurd notions
Benedict Arnolds with necks tired from pecking at the souls of their own people
From that sell out Negro named J. C. Watts
Swimming in conservative pots
Brought to a bubbling boil for his black skin
He doesn't even know that he's standing in
Tap dancing in
Prancing around with a sword of white teeth
cutting the chords attached to our advancement

Ward Connerly attempts to lay affirmative action down to rest
While the rest of Bush's cronies fail to protest
Uncle Tom Clarence Thomas puts his stamp of approval
                                    claiming it's for the best

Testing the existence of previous thoughts
They really think things have changed
All they've done is taken the shackles off our wrists
and put them on our brains
I wonder if they know that they've snatched the seeds of our dreams
and shoved them down our throats
Implanting weeds that will soon sprout out
and eclipse our brightest hopes

Republicans

Some**People**Don't**Need** A**Gun**To**Kill**You

They wouldn't stop bullying him
They picked and prodded away at his pride with knives of laughter
They thought that mess was funny
Took pleasure in seeing him fight back the tears,
They cheered at his misery
Seeing him get all choked up brought smiles to their faces
They all raced to see his lips quiver
See him get that lump in the back of his throat
They thought everything was meant to be nothing but a joke
But they just would never stop
It was like they couldn't get enough

A little push in front of your peers is a big deal
It's like they are stealing your joy
A meaningless trip
A stumble
A fall

They don't think it's that serious

Stuffing him in trash cans in the middle of the lunchroom for everyone to see
Or locking him in his own locker without giving anyone the key
He would want to yell but there would be no one there to listen
Or even care
He would stare at the teachers who would turn a blind eye
Pretending to be unaware

In bathrooms he would find himself head first in toilets
Dangling at the mercy of his enemies
A thousand flashlights couldn't find his dignity
It was forever lost like the cities of gold

Through public humiliation they murdered his pride
Abiding by the rules of the pecking order
Slaughtering his self worth as part of his soul died
Beating it black and blue
They were homicidal maniacs
Some people don't need a gun to kill you

He would walk the halls afraid waiting for the next attack
He knew any minute, it would arrive
Right on time, as if they were on a schedule
Unable to break the chain of events
He couldn't avoid the inevitable
Not even safe in his own skin, he began to hate the man in the mirror
Why did this cycle of hate have to continue
What did he do to deserve this
Why did they have to pick on him

Maybe they learned these techniques from people who once bullied them
A victim's curse
Unjustly suffering at the hands of those who have suffered
They invaded his territory
Pushing his pride to the west bank of his mind
With plans of erasing it from existence
Extermination
Displacements of their anger
Although he had nothing to do with the pain they endured,
it was returned to him 100 fold

His parents were too busy to notice anything was wrong
Singing the song of preoccupation
As long as he kept up his grades and stayed out of trouble, everything had to be
ok
Like a turtle he retreated into his shell
In hiding from the horrors of life
It was hard being a nobody
He remained unreachable

He wanted to take back his name in front of the entire school
Teach the world a lesson of respect
Next time they'll think twice about who they push around
He became consumed with violence like the Aztecs
With an uncontrollable anger like the Incredible Hulk
Growing hotter than the fire in his eyes and colder than the pain in his heart
Sparking thoughts of sweet revenge tickled his imagination
He wanted them to feel the burning sensation 1000 times
Pay for the crimes they committed against him

Their sticks and stones broke the bones of his soul
Their words stuck in his mind like a crown of thorns
Unable to shake them off like fleas
They murdered his dreams and hopes while their laughter butchered his happiness
He swore they would never call him a dork again
He had to pay them back
And he almost did
Luckily it didn't go any further than a bomb threat
All of this could have been avoided if someone would have paid attention
His parents
His teachers
His peers
Maybe they won't be so lucky next time

Or maybe his cries

his pain

and his anger

will be something
they'll actually

hear.

The**Know**It**All**

He thought he was so tough
rough and rugged around the edges
with a heart of
stone
A Lone Ranger that could break bones if he had to
Split domes if he's asked to
Bring terror to those who came at him sideways
His way or the highway was what he was used to
Quick tempered and hard headed
With a fuse shorter than Umpa Lumpas
You couldn't tell this kid nothing
Like a dude with a cheat sheet
He thought he had all the answers
Thought wisdom took over his body like cancer
And couldn't no preacher, teacher or parent tell him
what he already knew
And believe me they tried
They flooded his gates with advice
Their parental control units would spring to life like
pop up ads on AOL
But the truth of their words were just too hard to h ear
They were falling on deaf ears
He thought they switched gears to cramp his style
Knocking his hustle while pulling him down like crabs
in a barrel
Tattle telling on his every move
Longing for them to leave him the hell alone
To quit bombarding his mental with self-righteous
undertones
He couldn't see that everybody really loved him like
Raymond
He played himself like Othello taking advice
from the wrong people
Cats who he thought had vision like Coleco
Lethal injections of ignorance seemed to creep through
his peephole
Bad decisions ran sequels like trilogies
Hard headed like Nemo he found himself lost at sea
His future was poorly planned like post war strategies

He just didn't think it through
Unwilling to abandon his crew
He would follow them right over the cliff
Lifting each other into the fire together they would
piss away their dreams
Collectively lost like a mice in a maze trying to
find their way
Discovering nothing but dead ends
His Friends,
They would continue to bring him down like Bobby did
Whitney
He was determined to do what he wanted to do
Unwilling to apply himself in the classroom
Stupidity became the route he chose
His entire life was like one big door closing slow
And he couldn't even see it
For whatever reason, it just wasn't cool to study hard
He couldn't let anyone mistake him for being smart
Even though he was
He claimed self destruction as his mistress and let
the plethora of possibilities ooze out of him like puss
He had more chances than Dylan, but he just didn't
want to do right
He had all the potential in the world
Girl crazy and hard headed
His train of hope had long since derailed
Could have been anything in life he wanted to be
But instead
he rotts in a cell

Forgive them father for they know not what they do

—*Jesus*

Babies**having**babies

She hated looking in the mirror
Wrestling with a reflection she found offensive
Held without a connection to herself
Her features would keep her yearning for a change
Her self worth was maimed
Pride was currently out of commission
It was stained with disgust

The mirror was the enemy
Her eyes would stare with thoughts of disapproval
A constant removal of her felicity
Wanting to be born again
She yearned for the ability to go back in time like flex capacitors in a delorian
Modifying the flawed creation of her image
Contemplations of alterations would fill her dreams
Her hopes, and her desires

Boys ignored her
They ran from her like stockings
It was as if she had onion breath
The scent of a skunk
Or some sort of smell of death
Whatever the reason, they simply weren't interested
No one told her that true beauty comes from within

To get attention she started to wear less
Exposed to the benefits of being promiscuous

She thought that this could get her through
Thought she could ride this wave to conquer any hurdle life threw in her direction
Her body was her protection
Her shield
Her sword
Courting her suitors with a smile that would bring any man to their knees
Opportunities she seized
By any means
But she really short changed herself
Pigeonholed her dreams - setting the bar too low below her possibilities
The only assets she used were her physical abilities

So nobody ever really saw inside
Her mental potential was hidden like a code of Divinci
Unwilling to share her world like Mary J. Blidge
Her true self remained a buried treasure
Ten rulers couldn't measure the heights she should have climbed
She had to use what she had to get what she wants
Just too bad it wasn't her mind
She could shake it like Beyonce
Making heads turn til necks cracked
Exploring new realms like her first name was Ponce
De Leon style
Cats were quick to throw her smiles like menthos commercials
Attracting mack games like magnets
Was her everyday dress rehearsal
Making young minds think, "They had to have *this*"
Mini skirts, high heels, and way too much make up
was her only dedication
She created a stir
As her body was always the topic of conversation
Lil' Kim was her role model
Her way of life became her thesis
She left nothing to the imagination
Too many music videos had left her mind in pieces

She liked getting the attention
Satisfying raging hormones while causing dissension
in the midst of her morality
Her ethics were slipping like a broken transmission
Accepting demons of promiscuity to invade her reality
Two opposites would collide like Jekyll and Hyde cuz she really knew better
But pride was stinging at the side of her new found happiness
She didn't want to go back to being a nobody

So she continued
Offering a buffet of "whatevers" on her menu
She turned no one away
Service with a smile
Her doors were always open
Twenty four hours a day

She aimed to please
Left no one dissatisfied
Never even thought of the letters HIV
Statistics didn't scare her
And luckily, she missed that tragedy
But lurking around the corner
existed a different catastrophe
She got hit with a blitz
Never even saw it coming
Her belly starting swelling
It was too late to run to Mommy

She doesn't even understand her own body
Took her ten weeks to figure out what happened
Couldn't even calculate who was the baby's daddy

This disastrous calamity
No if ands or maybes
She's fifteen years old
A baby having a baby

The**Handshake**

She said my handshake offended her
That through this gesture I spat in her face and called her inferior
Sent her back in time to the suffrage movement
Banishing her to the line where castaways are forced to go
 Unequivocally downtrodden
Denied rights to be respected as a human being
Seen through patriarchal eyes
She told me to greet her like a woman, not like a lady
A firm handshake while looking her in the eye
Duplicated mental states of a jaded mind
Intrigued, I wanted to know more
She told me…

She was always treated with a fine tooth comb
Roaming through the pages of a fairy tale
She dreamed of her prince charming
Longing for a chariot
She set her bar as high as the heavens
Never allowing reality to creep into the depths of her mind
Through lessons of failed love she never found happiness
The method to her madness was shaped by craftiness
She dropped into the traps of the cunning fox time and time again
She fell for men's bodies ensnared in the minds of boys
Continued episodes of broken promises had stolen her joy
And now she had become a woman scorned

She wore her heart on her sleeve
She seized opportunities and welcomed possibilities with open arms
Suitors would charm her through methods of fascination
Impregnate her thoughts with feelings of captivation
She would be swept off her feet like Stella
Sent to ecstasy while trembles of passion would
hold her breath

          less

But she could never quite catch the carrot of her desires
She was constantly running a race that would refuse to end
Waiting in vain for a love that never came

Created a pain unable to mend her broken heart
Sending her spinning in circles of disappointment
With tired legs and a weary soul, she would continue to break down
Stuffed with over-exposed reels of Terry McMillian novels
that left her spellbound
All she wanted was a story book ending.
A constant state of waiting to exhale would cause her emotions to drown
Turning blue from the absence of air
The deaden stare of a cold cadaver
Her heart became an area of destitution
And she'll never look for love

in a man

again

Nightwalker

From the depths of nowhere I appear
Descending upon the earth as the sun discontinues to glow
The night walker

Responding to flashes of money, whistles and honked horns
Retreating to parked cars, back alleys and opened car doors
This is the life I chose
The street stalker

I exist as a prey in the middle of an open field in full view of my predator
Come and get me

The treasure between my legs isn't viewed as sacred,
it survives solely as a means to get by
This prized possession is handed out to anyone with the right dollar signs

Performing lewd acts in dark corners for the love of money
My soul is numb
I feel nothing

An**Abusive**Situation

He said she made him hit her
Because she wouldn't quit talking when he said to stop
And her lips kept flopping with wreckless abandonment
Ignoring his warnings to ceast and desist
She wouldn't discontinue her lyrical battles
Using words as her weapons to sharpen her voice
She sliced through his ego
Repeatedly stabbing his pride
Puncturing his wound with the irrational thinking seen through her eyes
The demise of his self pride was minimalized, as she chopped him down like cherry trees
But he made her pay
Everything comes with a price

Although he worshiped the ground she walked on
he could no longer see her angelic wings
She existed as a fallen angel
Growing a tail and horns with a venom spitting tongue
delivering 40 lashes to his soul
The blood of his spirit spewing out like a fountain

See, she was his backbone and his strength
She possessed the power to make him feel he could run through walls
Slaying any dragon that came in his path
That they were able to conquer the world together
Bonnie and Clyde style
The unbreakable bond

However, from dusk til dawn
A haze of miscommunication would fog their vision
Her woman's intuition should have seen this development
Pre-cog intelligence
She chose to ignore relevant indicators
Her third eye was blinded
Masked by some kind of mixture of ignorance, love, and fear
She couldn't hear the warnings that screamed at decibels
delivered at dangerously high volumes
They were falling on deaf ears
And as long as he would say that he's sorry, she would forgive him

Empty apologies flooded her gates
Time and time again
Her mirror would attempt to summon her intellect
Showing visual presentations that should have awakened her deceased soul
Her deadened spirit
Buried in a soil so deep that only wisdom and courage could reap
She's wise enough to size the situation and see it for what it is
But she doesn't
She can't bring herself to walk away

Why?
I can't wrap my fingers around the idea
I know she believes in heaven but she chooses to remain in hell
Being tortured by one of Satan's servants
She's smarter than this, I swear she is

Every time he loses his temper she sports sunglasses
to hide her prize fighter bruises
She wears scarfs in the summertime to cover marks that scarred her neck
The one he wrings like washrags
You can still see the imprints from his fingers from where his grip held her breathless
Caressing her throat with a choking connection
His hands soaked with her tears

He cracks a smile like a rotwieller
A vampire
Ready to sink his teeth into the depths of her soul
Sucking out the life that once ran rampant throughout her body
Sending her octaves higher like helium
He deflated her happiness
Popped it like blood blisters
Covering her with sinister actions
Smothering her with blankets of physical transactions
Right hooks, backhands, and jabs
Fully clothed with blows and bruises that abundantly stained her body
Violating her temple's hall
Lips were split like decisions

He left his tag on her wall
Cupped hands muffled her swollen mouth so her screams would go unheard
Her self worth was gone with the wind
Twirling in a tunnel of inner loathing

She had become one of those blow up dolls that you hit to the floor
And just as fast as they went down, pop back up asking for more
She would see him in her dreams
Krueger style
Hearing knuckles crack like a glove of knives raked across a chalkboard
The very thought would make her jump in her skin
Terrified replays that haunted her unconscious
What had she become?
A never ending torture chamber
A precious candle with a broken wick
A beautiful bird with a broken wing
Unable to pretend that this madness will ever end
But worse than that
To this very day

She's still with him

True**Friendship**

Through pensive eyes he contemplated speaking
Seeking some type of refuge from the war within
His mind was spinning like his thoughts
Meditated migraines
He sought a mental asylum
His spirit was drowning in pools of denial
Life preservers were scarce
Unable to be found through search parties headed by bloodhounds of liberation
He remained in captivity
He felt as though zoo keepers have kept him locked behind the key of life
Denied him access to the kingdom called happiness
And now, he dwelled in darkness

Through his eyes I saw fear
It rung like levels of base piercing the drums of my ears
Through water filled eyes he tried to keep the rivers from flowing
Behind an invisible dam, not one tear dropped

The lump in his throat would wrestle his words
Concerned with my reaction
his speech patterns would retreat to the depths of his passion
Living in the land of lost language
A lowered level of linguistic communication
For when he opened his mouth, nothing came out
Just a deep breath as heavy as the weight on his heart

Through clenched fists I could see his rage
A caged animal yearning to be set free
His features showed flashes of torment
For I could see him walking through the dangers
of a never-ending torture chamber
His soul looked bruised
Sparking my interest I longed to know the topic of conversation
What could possibly be this serious?

More Than An Athlete

He hesitated before forcing the words out of his mouth
He said he was tired of hiding
Cowering in the closet of the truth
Like a scared animal
Afraid of the horrors that lie on the other side
Waiting for his demise
Screams were showering his thoughts
He could hear the voice of his father shouting from the mountain tops

THIS AIN'T THE WAY THAT MEN FEEL!!!

Although it was instilled since days of adolescence
the feeling he had he just couldn't conceal
Through murderous plots this feeling he would try to kill
A feeling not even time could heal

He told me that he had been on a journey
With flashlights of exemption he yearned to emancipate his soul
Let loose form the shackles of society that bound him at the feet
Handcuffed to reality
They beat him with batons of normalcy
Attempts to chase the son of the morning out of his earth
Throwing scriptures like darts hoping they would stick

Mentally abused
They used every angle to mangle his thoughts
In their eyes, he dwelled in a state of confusion
They yearned to untangle the web in which he was caught
Casting stones of condemnation
Bewildered at how their son could partake in episodes of abomination
He felt disowned
His friends dropped him
Like this was a disease they could catch if they stood too close
Everyone turned on him, and now he was all alone

At first I felt betrayed
Thinking back to sleep-overs and the sharing of sodas
I couldn't see how this could happen to someone so close to me
Nothing against them but that just wasn't my thing
I've known him for what seemed forever
"About going pro," we dreamed together
Shared our most inner secrets
Hell, we taught each other about the birds and the bees
The blind leading the blind
He knew things about me
no one else knew

With him
I would share my fears
No fight for him would I ever back down
For years and years we've had each other's back
What kind of friend would I be
if I didn't have it now?

Can you see the pride of the panther? As she nurtures her young all alone. The seed must grow, regardless of the fact that it's planted in stone

—*Tupac Shakur*

Alone

He left her all alone
A woman on a raft in the middle of the ocean
Wrestling options of abortion
She really didn't have much of a choice
Those wet thoughts melted in the palm
of her desire for a
family

She wanted her picket fence!
Ever since Barbie dolls, she's had this dream
She wanted to be a part of the team
Making matrimonial bonds
Jumping brooms in white dresses
Walking with her groom arm and arm
Hearing the familiar sound of marital songs

She wanted baby showers with her closest friends and family
So she could eat cucumber sandwiches with the crust cut off
But, none of that would happen

The light of her dreams, shut out by blinders
Eclipsed by clouds of reality
A constant reminder that her desires refused
to glow in the dark

she deserved better

He said:

"He would always be there for her
That she was his queen!

Who he couldn't imagine life without her because

she
completed his soul
The missing part to the puzzle of his life that made him whole
He claimed her mere existence was more precious than gold
He called her

his rib

His reason for breathing
Said he would feel the pain of a baby teething
when she would leave his presence

In essence, she was his everything

And she believed him
Hung on his every word
Felt comfort in his ability to care for her
With him
she felt safe

Laced with security
She was his prize placed gently in the manger of his heart
Kick starting her desire to make them last forever
He said she was the "sweetest thing he'd ever known"
That he would become overwhelmed at the sight of her glow!

His breath would escape him
The constant tick of his clock reminding him
of his never ending love
by the hour

Until the test came back positive
The thought of a third addition
Flashed into their picture of life

She never knew
he could run so fast

He was a delectable taste
Quickly turned sour
The biggest mistake in her life
was falling in love
with a coward

Trust

She said that she loved him
But she just couldn't trust him

She had dreams of him linked to foreign hemispheres
Entranced into the arms of another
She searched his back for fingerprints but found none
Imaginations of conjured up infatuations saturated her mental patterns
Thoughts are twirling like dancers inside her head
Harassing the possibilities until the cops come knocking
Creating a stoppage in her flow of trust
Her accusations pierce the side of his soul
Her questions, stinging darts

She might as well put the knife in his heart with her own hands
Unable to travel to foreign lands
She's stuck in ancient quick sands of doubt
Unable to stand tall in security
She's shouted for someone to save her from drowning
Thoughts around her are circling
Maybe he is the one destined for crowning a queen
and teaching her how to swim

Brighten possibilities once dim
Simplifying matters once impossible for her mind to stem
She's been bitten once too many times by snakes that slithered in and out of her
existence and left footprints on her heart
Holding on to past indiscretions
And keeping them for her private collection
Tucked away for future reference
Unable to cast her election
In fear of falling from flight
Unable to fly with wings held by the strength of confidence
She remains with both feet planted firmly on the ground
Taking refuge in pools of doubt
Peddling through rivers of uncertainty
Stopping the continuity of her flow
In fact, her flow was blocked like contraceptive sponges
She's swung lower than chariots
No wonder she can't seem to keep from drowning

The world of her unconscious hounds her from sun up to sun down
Sending rivers
Of unanticipated shivers
Making her sea sick
How could she stay above surface?

He was almost at his wick's end
He was growing tired of being blamed for shameless acts
If he was father time
He would turn back the hands of crimes
that have crippled her daily walk
Forming another bad creation
Without hesitation
He would give her the key to unlock her prisoner of trust
Held captive in her mind's recollection
He would bust through the gates with guns a blazing
Shooting bullets of love and passion to pierce her damaged heart
Reviving a beat once found between the rhythms of his mind
They would be able to intertwine a connection like one they'd never seen
Instead of him paying for crimes, blackening his eye
With crushing blows delivered from a dangerously mistrusting mind

His desires flicker on and on like neon signs
But the truth keeps creeping into the window of his existence
Thieves in the night
Tapping on his lids
Pirates, hijacking the truth
Opening the blinds which once eclipsed his mind
Shadowing reality from the view of his path

She doesn't trust based on her own deception

Now he saw the truth clearly
Without trust
What did they really have?

Karma

Thoughts crawling over his mind like ants on bread crumbs
Creeping into the nightmare of his dreams like elm street
Plucking the strings of his imagination with contagious viruses infecting the
circumference of his thoughts
He's nervous...

He's having visions, running through his mental like electric currents
Stagnating the blood flowing from his heart, causing it to skip a beat
Held short of breath, stuck at the peak of a roller-coaster
Looking down at what lies ahead
Eyes wide open
Holding on for dear life

Through the duration of his relationship he's been monogamously challenged
Held captive to handicapped passions leading him astray
Mesmerized by foreign thighs
He couldn't stay away from temptation
The Call Of The Wild
Howling at the sight of the full moon
The hounds of lust would leave him spellbound
Consumed with desire
Annihilated mind states of restraint
He just couldn't say no
Enticed by the thought of seduction...

His patterns were scarred by fathers of infidels
For they authored his book of life
Mirrored atrocities
He followed paths of the unrighteous
Roads commonly traveled
Standards were crossed eyed, double vision
Boarding the unfaithful enterprise
He was beamed up like Scottie
In his eyes, he didn't stand a chance

The word no would scarcely visit his crown
Refusing to turn down offers
Mere smiles would leave him spellbound

Entranced like hypnotized minds
Following the switching of backsides
Would send a burning inside the depths of his infatuation
Mental pictures couldn't stop the penetration of his sewn desires
below his waist
His inquisitive mind wanted to know
Curious as a cat
His loins would be burning
On fire from his yearning to plunge into the caves of foreign territory
He existed as every players dream
A living allegory telling the story of a man not trustworthy

So many women, so little time
In abundance of variety, shape, and size
Drawing conclusions to rationalize his actions
He even pulled out Solomon having 500 wives
As disloyal as they are, his oats have been sewn
For he's blown through enough caverns for ten men
Crawled through the crevice of clandestine magnitudes
He was really on the DL
Low down like dirty dogs he stayed in heat
Inflamed with passion that seeped through the cracks of monogamy
He covered his tracks like cats in litter
He defiled his relationship many moons prior
It was almost like he didn't care
Or maybe, he was just trying to fool himself

But from the depths of his mind
a feeling would begin to arise
He would disguise his own fears
Steering clear of the thoughts telling him
she would be well within her right
What goes around comes around
He knew what he deserved and
it ate him up inside

"Africa to me is more than a glorious fact. It is a historical truth. No man can know where he is going unless he knows exactly where he has been and exactly how he arrived at his present place."

—Maya Angelou

Return**Of**The**Warrior**

Back in the day when I used to roam free
Before subjugators injected their evil into my veins
I would seek to entertain my thoughts with mathematical contemplation
Calculations of physics led to the creation of the pyramids
The burden of proof existed in the face of the sphinx
As Napoleon grew fonder of my style
Jealous of my intellect
I remained proud
I didn't have to "say it loud"
It rang at high decibels with my every existence
It was a shining bright star in the eyes of my people
Forever glowing with persistence
My mind possessed the eternal flame
That burned at scorching hot levels
Able to differentiate between angels and devils
I was never fooled
But I schooled my young with the knowledge of self
The intellect of their ancestors that passed on generations of wisdom
The kingdoms that came
The wills that were done
On earth as they were in heaven
I had seven days a week to reign on my throne
My heart pumped with the power of a warrior
I rejoiced like the birth of Simba
As my young entered into manhood
Armed with a shield of immortality among mortals
My women remained on pedal stools
As the atmosphere surrounding their every existence shouted the elegance of a queen
Words spoken but not seen was never the case in this place of history
And like the hands on a clock
My mind was forever turning
Manifesting ideas into realities
The queen of the Nile bore witness to Cleopatra
The essence of ebony remained in tact
Until...
A ship of human cargo left the western shores of my sand
I lost my warrior stance while dwelling in a serpent's land
No longer did my reflection signify the beauty of the florescent moon
A herd of wild boor infested my temple

But I'm still seeking the knowledge of self
The self love once held captive between the minds of my ancestors
I'm climbing to heights unknown
Rising above the blissful state of ignorance
While searching for the resurrection of my people
My shield of intellect is warding off the attacks of superiority
The Jesus I know looks like me
I don't know who that white man in the picture is
Minds are blessed with the fortification of truth
Providing substance to a withering spirit
Enabling the intellectual growth of a people searching for a way out
Styles are incorrect
Minds are lop-sided
And cock eyed
Apparently the circle of life has discontinued the pursuit of happiness
That once ran deeper than baby dimples
Spirits have been popped like pimples
Creating tidal waves in our vision
Inserting incisions of self doubt
Sending minds on routes of false prophesies
Confusing intellectual stabilities like the mysteries of the earth
Proceeding with caution on a tight rope of self worth
Cuz knowledge is what I'm seeking
But ignorance is right there
Like nightmares
Catching my people while their sleeping
Crawling through the cracks in the wall like roaches
When it rains it pours
But I'm still soaring like an eagle
My eyes are still set on sights
Of climbing to new heights
Too high for oppressors to reach
Minds I wish to enhance
I'll stand tall with pride
When I regain my warrior's stance

BringOur**Heroes**Home

Out of the ashes of Iraq come soldiers dressed in fatigues of fire
Wearing helmets secured in smoke
They've choked off the lies spewed out of the mouth of a burning bush
The true warrior's inevitable wake
Who's flames burned them at the stake
Cremated their bodies
And stuffed them in an urn wrapped in red, white, and blue

Rummaging through a forest set ablaze by one lethal match
With witty catch phrases forever attached to the side of their kingdom

Operation Iraqi Freedom
Links to Al Qaeda
Eminent threats
And weapons of mass destruction

They've searched for the point where the truth echoes
in the distance
and can be heard for miles
Where skies are filled with the blue of the ocean
Birds are abundant, flopping their wings through the smiles of spring
The existence of their freedom
in disguise

The essence of their happiness
cloaked in a web of lies
As far as their eyes can see
They're doomed

They've been skillfully thrown into the lion's den
Out of the frying pan and into the furnace
Their courage exceeds any measuring stick

For they've been led into the eye of the storm
Transformed into peacekeepers
Lending a helping hand for the poorly planned post-war strategy
Like the dolphin
Held captive in a foreign net
Caught in a web of circumstance

Not made for tuna-like consumptions
With dreams of freedom clouding their memories
Whispering nickel-plated nursery rhymes in their ear
A dehydrated oasis
They remember their past, but their present haunts their daily prayers
They feel the stares of resentment
The eyes of disdain continue to stain their canvas of hope
Their mission was to rope freedom through lassos of liberation
To bind an evil dictator and give birth to democracy
But perception has nothing to do with reality

Over there
They're seen as the enemy
Strangers in a strange land
Unwanted guests invading sands
foreign to the truth
They exist as walking targets
A bulls eye painted onto the middle of their fatigues
Suicide bombers that will gladly give their lives to destroy their existence
With casualties piling higher than the deficit
The rest of it doesn't seem to be looking any brighter
They have to drink the deadly cocktail of anti-American bombs
Bullets fall like rain

They over there plotting
Like The Count Of Monte Cristo waiting for the right time to strike

Using our soldiers   as pawns
to get closer   to conquering

this kingdom called democracy

Lack of post-war planning
Produced a chaotic situation
The future looks dimmer than the opinions of this strategy
Assaults are bombarding our troops like bombs over Baghdad
Progress is moving at a snail's pace
While our soldiers run a race against time

The clock keeps ticking against their lifelines
Who in their right mind would continue
the crime
of holding them hostage?

The deafening tone of death counts shivers our bones
As we roam through the morning pages of injustice

Enough is enough
Please, bring our heroes home

Cockroaches

I'm trying to get rid of these cockroaches
These black cockroaches
Crawling all over my freedom
Existing as a weight pressing against my progression
Dimming the beacon of light seen through a peephole of opportunity
Staining the flesh of my people
Continuing sequels raining down pain like melodies from heaven
Me being me, Black, Proud and destined to be free can plainly see my enemy
and not all have pale faces.
I can't seem to find that brotha of mine that once existed in the multitudes
See I gotta be watching my back for massu's whip that was handed down to
hands that resemble mine
They might look like me
Have features like me
And maybe even smell like me
But when they look in the mirror, they don't see me
They see extensions of their enemy tied in knots
I'm talking about cockroaches like J. C. Watts
Throwing rocks at the throne of our advancement
Enhancing his resume by stepping on his people
Absorbing evil traditions into his mind like a sponge
Fueling a fire already burning for our souls
The color of a conservative should not look like you
Not Larry Elder, Armstrong Williams
But you're just as confused as Uncle Tom Clarence Thomas
Who I shouldn't even waste time on
However, it's a crime on top of a crime
Bush picked you to replace a man whose shoes are too big for you to fill
You could've been an injection of Thurgood Marshall into the veins of society
An extension of the pride he instilled in the side of Black souls
Standing up for causes that caused white hoods in white robes
to turn over in their grave
Shook up the world with turbulence
But you are not on that level!
Trading thoughts and ideas with devils
You're doing your *Bo jangles Shuffle* on the Supreme Court
Jumping up and down, waving your hand to volunteer
to take the stick from master's hands and beat
the slaves with it yourself

Claiming you pulled up your own bootstraps
But Bush pushed you right into the seat
Able to leap past unqualified proportions
Your self loathing runs deep
Clipping your brainwashed ideas onto the hips of our justice
And Anita should have smacked you in your sell out lips
The disrespectful antagonist
Instead of standing on your feet you grovel like a coward on your knees
A pathetic excuse for a man
Which brings me to Alan Keys
The carpetbagger from Maryland
Allowing yourself to be used as a token
The well spoken crumb snatcher
Catching the leftovers from his master's table
Able to assimilate the ways of the wicked
You exist as their identical twin
Running a race you'll never win
But you're too blinded to see
An Obama you will never beat
You're too busy doing the devil's work like Ward Connerly
And as far as Collin Powell and Condaleeza Rice
You're both leaders of great stature but don't steer us down the wrong path
Don't succumb to beliefs absent from your intelligent minds
You know the difference between what's right and wrongful crimes
If the words you speak are not your beliefs do not speak them as though they are

The next time you pick a side make sure you think it through
Or the next poem I write might be about you

The**Murder**that**Murder**Produced
(The Penalty is Death)

Making sure cats don't get the chance to atone for crimes
These methodologies have been used since the beginning of time
By people in power with a God complex
Once held in check by his son
Telling the people " He who is without sin to cast the first one"
Stones used to be the weapon of choice but now they use lethal injections

Protection from the masses in the form of execution?
An eye for an eye is your solution?

You feel justified in murdering people who murder people
to show that murdering people is wrong?

Singing that song of what's good for the goose is good for the gander
Scandalous barbarians enforcing evil traditions
What makes you think the death by lethal injection is any less sadistic
then the gas chamber or public hangings
Firing squad or the electric chair
Being stoned to death

The Guillotine or the Crucifix?

What gives you the right to decide
Who deserves to die and who doesn't?
If you keep playing God, the real one might get mad
Only He knows
He judges the ways of the wicked

Still, you continue to try to do God's job
You are not on that level
A devil posing as an angel but I see through your disguise
Your horns are protruding through your conservative lies
Don't think that your thirst for blood doesn't translate to my ultimate demise
I'm not dumb deaf or blind
I've seen your handy-work over the course of time
I've been permanently stained by the blood dripping from your fangs
Let's visit a crime scene where Black men with broken necks
bore witness to your idea of justice
Nooses grace the necks of my memory
Reminding me constantly
But I'll always see clearly

More Than An Athlete

You are in no position to accuse anybody of anything
But still you do

Breakthroughs in DNA rescue brothas from your grasp
Wrongly accused faster than the speed of your lies travel
Unraveling facts ignored by frightened eye witnesses
Sentencing resting on the tongues of white Memphis Bells
since the times of Emmett Till

If I can afford my freedom, I'll just buy it
But, what if you're poor?

I don't know if he did it or not....
But rest assured if O.J. wasn't rich he would be on death row
right now counting down his days
Even with that racist Mark Furman
or the questionable handling of the evidence reality
Statistics tell me that when a Black man is accused of killing two white people
The penalty is death.
The rich are allowed to swim to the surface
while the poor are left drowning in an abyss of hopelessness

Tell me how many court appointed attorneys discover
                              ways to prevent wrongful convictions?

For every O.J. there are 100 Mumias
Sitting on death row awaiting their time of execution
Watching the clock tick the minutes of their lives away
Treated as an open and shut case
without being found guilty
beyond the shadow of a doubt

Imagine being on trial for a crime you didn't commit
Not allowed to represent yourself but forced to put your life in the hands of some
unqualified public defendant who doesn't even believe you're innocent
Watch him stumble over poorly prepared notes
While gazing at a jury of none of your peers
Already attacking you with dismal sneers of
disdain and distrust
No financial resources means no fair trial.

Now you've tried to extend your songs of slaughter to include:
Women/the mentally retarded/and children

You're an equal opportunity killer
Nesting eggs of destruction to
birth newborns of restless corruption

The murder that murder produced

By the time we catch up to justice we'll be out of breath
Left gasping for a freedom

We could only dream of

"I don't have to be what you want me to be, I'm free to be who I want to be.
—*Muhammad Ali*

Don't**Think**I**Forgot**

The Land Of Milk and Honey
The Land Of Opportunity

People jump on rafts
         in the middle of the night
                just for the chance
to land
safely on the borders

They risk their lives for a taste of the freedoms we enjoy here
While we do have our share of problems
Truly we are blessed

But don't think I forgot

The whips and chains that have permanently stained my history
The dark cloud that hung its ugly head over our existence
Casting a shadow of oppression
to cease the resurrection of our mind and spirits
Body and soul
The replayed recreation of sinister plots
evil schemes
heartless deeds
that locked our wrists together in shackles of despair
wallowing in the pit of subjugation
the devil's economic plan to rise to greatness on the backs of my forefathers
off the sweat of their brow
the pain of their suffering
the extent of their misery

Please Don't Think I Forgot

The mutilated bodies hanging from trees like chandeliers
blood stained nooses dangling lifeless bodies like castrated figurines
they violated temples more precious than gold
exhibiting the mastery of savages raping the mind, body and soul

Please Don't Think I Forgot

The underwater graveyards
the ocean of bones that cover the bottom of the sea
the trail of remains that line the middle passage

 More Than An Athlete

heartless men who threw human lives
over the sides of slave ships
discarded like garbage into a sea of sharks

the murderous thieves
violated dreams of forced migration
branded as cattle, they mutilated our souls
packed like sardines
we existed as human cargo
mere chattel
kidnapped treasures
goods to be bought and sold

Please Don't Think I Forgot

Dred Scott's decision still haunts my memory
the resurfaced audacity
the god complex of white supremacy
claiming your clan to be purebred pedigree descendancy
giving birth to a nation of imbeciles

claiming Africans were only 3/5ths of a human
and the Missouri Compromise as unconstitutional

I wonder how they slept at night?
how the wickedness of their deeds didn't paint pictures of horror scenes
how their conscious didn't bloody their souls
or break the backbones of their spirits

and they called themselves Christians
men who lack a conscious will even lie to themselves

Please Don't Think I Forgot

Medgar Evars and Cointelpro
Police dogs and their Water Hoses
The Tulsa Race Riots and white only stalls
Willie Lynch and the Fugitive Slave Laws
The Birth Of A Nation
J. Edgar Hoover and James Earl Ray
The beastly raping our women/the auction block/ the beatings/the torture/the
breeding/the branding and Bloody Sunday

Slave names
Public hangings
Malcolm and Martin
Segregation
The Civil Rights Struggle
We Shall Overcome
Confederate Flags
Mississippi Burning
Hooded cowards hiding behind sheets
Jim Crow
The Back Of The Bus

"We didn't land on Plymouth Rock, Plymouth Rock landed on us"

Burning Crosses
4 Little Girls
Lil' Bobby Sutton and the Infiltration of the Panthers
Harriet Tubman and the Underground Railroad
Uncle Tom's Cabin and Kunta Kente
The slave ships
Amistad and Cinque
Nat Turner
Denmark Vecey
Marcus Garvey
Huey P. Newton
Assata Shakur
and Emmett Till

Please Don't Think I Forgot

Because I haven't
and I never will

A State of **War***

Aftermath of destruction sparks newfound discernment
Heard the wind blow through the treetops
The North Star is burning

In the streets, the paper chase has lowered a veil
And each nation is keeping its greatest leaders in jail

What a time to return, resurrected in the sand
Tarnish the name of freedom to exercise my plan
The ballot is a shackle, a leader without a fan
A legal lynching is swung by the executive branch

See, I was born from out the belly of the sweat from the field
Brotherhood was the bond that his jealousy killed
The sword kept my hunger supreme
gun powder snuck from the east
Disrupt the present in the air that you breathe

I wrote the topic when they chopped the map of Africa's shores
Slayed the Natives with the syphilis of European whores
Camouflaged in the likeness of truth
a guillotine is my tooth
Nuked Japan and almost wiped out the Jews
Took up the tactics of guerillas
when the jungle was lost
I brought the thunder to the desert
bombing churches and mosques
Innocent lives were taken
the banner is stepping clear
They'll never understand my greatest weapon is fear
Some say the seventh seal will open like the flash of a gun
They tell my love can not be stolen
but I'll blast it and run

Remastered the plunge
free falling like addicts for
fun

More Than An Athlete

I'll make a ruthless paratrooper
out your first born son
Fresh outta graduation, aiming at that first million
A twisted capsule shot the shrapnel through his grill
and was done

Took his eyes from the hairs of the cross in hesitation
The moment was lost, and now his lungs are suffocating

Grasping the finger of a friend from class
he collapsed to the grass
And I just sat back and laughed

Squadrons are armed with a vengeful force
See the comrades carving out a lion's roar
Thought he had the game won, caught him with a flame gun
My name out your mouth and we'll keep this hit the same son
Label me a psycho, travel as the night blows
Tattoo on my chest is an automatic riffle
Veterans will die slow, money is my cycle
Took my overhead just to fund the spread of white blow

Governments been using me, genocide ain't new to me
Young people stay high, then go be all that you could be
Unemployed recruitment, that's how I get you sent
From the liquor store, now you scrubbing floors at
boot camp
Mind control is dominant, allegiance I want all of it
Took religion's hand, now we're forming a conglomerate
Terror brought me prominence
tragic like the towers that fall
You keep your greatest enemy the closest of all
I set the court for black crime
that's how I attack minds
Send them overseas, and that's fifty brothers flatline
Realize, victory or death the world is mine
Its like a jungle sometimes

—   *Poem by guest poet, Julian Thomas*

HowAmIWorthy?

At what point do apologies become meaningless?
Repentance become obsolete
No matter how much I sin
I'm always be forgiven
Dwelling in an abundance of failures
I still call myself a Christian
But how Christ like am I
By his stripes I've been healed
But I still feel afflicted
Convicted like felons
I continue to fall off the path to righteousness

It's like walking on a tight rope
With an elephant sized weight on my back
A balancing act
Weighing on me like I'm Atlas
Holding the weight of my salvation on my shoulders
With my lifetime to practice
Walking through the valleys of the shadows of death
Should I fear the evil that dwells inside me?
And around me
And through me
And over me
It's abundantly clear like present danger
This stranger is no stranger to me
Being present since the beginning of humanity
Evil plays the world like an instrument
It blows through me as moistened lips through a flute
A lifetime orchestra
With acute sounds that punctuate my soul
Wrapping around it like an anaconda
Slithering through the grass of my existence
Biting apples of foretold consequences
Destined to birth newborns wrapped in blankets of sin
A heavenly curse
Dwelling from within the depths of the scriptures
Encoded for my better understanding
A nagging injury that tends to linger throughout the course of my lifeline
With fingers massaging oil of doubt into the bosom of mankind
Can I continue this race?

Run its course without losing to pulled hamstring of failure
Or am I the metamorphasized rabbit chasing a carrot that I'll never reach?
The road to hell is paved with good intentions
Not to mention
The lake of fire that liars are destined to swim laps in
And if I just happen to fall asleep before I get the chance to say amen
I'm still on bended knees
Pleading for your grace to fall on my face like raindrops
I am Donnie Maclurklin's sinner that keeps falling down
But how many rounds can I go until I am finally counted out
Disqualified or technically knocked out
I know that the scripture says that you'll be forgiven
as many times as you ask for forgiveness
But is it possible to wear God out?
I've shouted to the heavens above to make me
Break me into molded pieces of clay
Forming the steadfast spirit of Job
I've never been tested to that level
But the devil keeps knocking at my door
He keeps creeping into the cracks of my faith
Communicating through subliminal messages invading my soul
I know if you resist the devil he will flee
But what will keep him away
Obstacles keep popping up like dandelions
Upon crossing one hurdle, there's 5 more lurking
around the corner of my strength
It mirrors images of conquered spirits
So I stay on guard
Making sure I bob and weave through the thrust of temptations
Your word is my "souls detergent"
Washing away the impurities that have stained me
Corrupted me/entrusted me with the ability to falter
How can I lay my burdens down at the alter of your forgiveness
when I know that I will fall again
Knees scabbed from a never ending plunge
I'm not where I should be
But I'm better than where I was

Poems**I**have**n't**gotten**a**chance**to**write**yet**

1. The Palestinian/ Israeli conflict

2. With everything that he's done, how can he possibly get re-elected for four more years?

3. Bin Laden
   a. Maniac terrorist?
   b. Jealous of our way of life?
   c. A business deal gone bad?
   d. The chickens coming home to roost?

4. The Fans
   First they love you, then they hate you, then they love you again

5. What can happen when you drive drunk

6.
   a.Why nobody cares about what Jesus was doing from age 12-30
   b. Why certain books were left out of the Bible

   c. Why religion has been used as the greatest weapon this country has ever seen
   d. What difference would it make if Jesus had a wife?

7. Bill O'Reily, Sean Hannity and Ann Coulter

8. The future of gangstas
   a. A funeral
   b. A Prison

9. A message to Colin Powell
   (It's time for you to speak the truth)

10. Is the NCAA (Athletics) a few steps above slavery?

11. The Patriot Act

12. Virginia

13. The NRA

Anytime there is a self-loving, self-respecting, self-determining Black Man, he is one of the most dangerous folks in America. Because it means you are free enough to speak your mind, you're free enough to speak the truth

—*Cornell West*

Publisher'sNote

When I first started Moore Black Press in 1997, I took a leap of faith. In my one bedroom apartment in Brooklyn, I enlisted the help of my closest artist friends and decided to do something novelist and playwright T. Tara Turk always talked about - black writers and artists actually leaving something behind. Some proof of our history, through paint, film, photography, music, theater and of course, words inside books.

My *Showtime at the Apollo* appearance quickly became a part of my immediate history, and I began a mission of proving to the New York City "literati" that I was a serious poet and writer, not just playing one on TV. I was an admirer of my talented peers and took my generation of poets and writers quite serious. Everyone reading poems in new york in 1995 knew something special was happening with poetry and I was excited to be a part of the history. A dear friend and angel, Weldon Irvine, whispered in my ear at a panel discussion at The Schomberg Center for Black Research in Harlem some years ago. He told me that I was the only artist on the panel with anything relevant for him to listen to because I actually owned my own art. He also told me publishing was a thankless job.

There are many choices I've made since finding my own voice in poetry. Publishing Etan Thomas is one of my most important. Etan represents everything that Moore Black Press is about. Fearlessness, stepping outside of your comfort zone, taking risks, ownership, tradition, independence, definition, a celebration of our culture, our history, our literature, our struggles, our stories. What we do with language as poets is magic and science, skill and spirit. As Black poets, we are challenged with telling the truth and exploring our oppression as survivors. 2005 is an important year for MBP and the incredible voices joining Etan Thomas in believing in Moore Black Press is an accomplishment already. I am honored and humbled to be in such great company. So, in this world of people forgetting to say thank you. Thank you Etan and all my poets, friends, staff (Patrick), interns, ancestors and family (especially my beautiful husband Kenyatta) for helping to make the first 8 years possible, and the future even more powerful.

We continue
In the tradition
of legacy.

jessica Care moore-Poole
Publisher

Other**books**from
mooreblack**press**

Bestsellers

The Words Don't Fit In My Mouth by jessica Care moore-Poole
ISBN# 0-9658308-0-2   Paperback; 145 pages, poetry

The Seventh Octave by Saul Williams
ISBN# 0-9658308-1-0   Paperback; 55 pages, poetry

Fast Cities and Objects That Burn by Sharrif Simmons
ISBN# 0-9658308-29   Paperback; 76 pages, poetry

The Alphabet Verses The Ghetto by jessica Care moore-Poole
ISBN# 0-9658308-7X   Paperback; 155 pages, poetry

Forthcoming Titles:

The Subtle Art of Breathing by asha bandele
ISBN# 0-9658308-8-8

Black Girls Love Hard by Ras Baraka
ISBN#0-9658308-5-3

The Poetry of Emcees: An Anthology of Hip Hop Generation writers known to
rock the pen. Edited by jessica Care moore-Poole
ISBN#0-9658308-4-5

God is Not An American by jessica Care moore-Poole
ISBN#0-9658308-6-1   Hardcover; poetry and essays

A Novel by T. Tara Turk.

mooreblacknotes

_____
_____
_____
_____
_____
_____
_____
_____
_____
_____
_____
_____
_____
_____
_____
_____
_____
_____
_____
_____
_____
_____
_____
_____
_____
_____
_____
_____

Discography

Intro/My Heritage/How Am I Worthy?/My First Love
Toys 'R' Us Kid/Wasted Talent*/Haters/An Abusive Situation
A Field Trip/The Murder That Murder Produced/Republicans
The "N" Word/Some people don't need a gun to kill you
Don't think I forgot/Bring Our Heroes Home
Return of The Warrior/The State of War/Outro

More Than An Athlete: *The Experience*

The Executives: Kenyatta Poole, Etan Thomas and jessica Care moore-Poole
The Producer and Arranger: Kenyatta Poole

The Poet: Etan Thomas
The Vocalist: Mrs. Nichole Thomas
Guest Poet: Julian Thomas
*Produced by Beats By The Minute

The Players:

Suga Cookie - Drums
Ryan Waters - Guitar
JaJa Dessauer - Bass
Skippy- Guitar
Val Parker - Keyboards
LaTonya Peoples - Violin
Ron James - Saxophone
Milkshake Mayfield- Trumpet
Poetry Intro - featuring Mrs. Poole

Recorded at Patchwerks Studio and STR
Mixed and Mastered at STR Studios
by Scott Thomas and Kenyatta Poole
6 - 4 - 19
To contact Kenyatta Poole: mooreblackpress@yahoo.com

More Than An Athlete